POEMS: NEW & SELECTED

Writings by Jane Joritz-Nakagawa

BOOKS

Skin Museum (Avant Books, 2006)
Aquiline (Printed Matter Press, 2007)
EXHIBIT C (Ahadada Books, 2008)
The Meditations (Otoliths, 2009)
incidental music (BlazeVOX, 2010)
notational (Otoliths, 2011)
FLUX (BlazeVOX, 2013)
Distant Landscapes (theenk Books, 2015)
<<terrain grammar>> (theenk Books, 2018)

CHAPBOOKS

wildblacklake (Hank's Original Loose Gravel Press, 2014)
diurnal (Grey Book Press, 2016)

EBOOK

terra form[a] (Argotist Ebooks, 2017)

EDITOR

women: poetry: migration [an anthology] (theenk Books, 2017)

Poems: New & Selected

Jane Joritz-Nakagawa

selected by Paul Rossiter
foreword by Eric Selland

ISOBAR
PRESS

First published in 2018 by

Isobar Press
Sakura 2-21-23-202, Setagaya-ku,
Tokyo 156-0053, Japan
&
14 Isokon Flats, Lawn Road,
London NW3 2XD, United Kingdom

https://isobarpress.com

ISBN 978-4-907359-25-6

Poems copyright © Jane Joritz-Nakagawa 2018
Foreword copyright © Eric Selland 2018

All rights reserved.

ACKNOWLEDGEMENTS

Thanks to the editors of *A glimpse of*, *Marsh Hawk Review* and *Wordgathering*, where parts of *Plan B Audio* were first published. Cover image: *Fuji Sunrise Spring 2016h* by Marcus Grandon © Marcus Grandon 2018. Author photograph by Junichiro Nakagawa.

Contents

Foreword: Eric Selland / 11

NEW

from *Plan B Audio* (work in progress)

'courtship of empty space' / 17
'paramount desert' / 18
'a portmanteau of crimes' / 19
'liquid determination' / 20
'greying sky' / 21
'Impossible collapsing dialogues evict' / 25
'why not   swoon if' / 27
'implanted deep in the breasts of all' / 28

§

& SELECTED (2006–2017)

poems from *Skin Museum* (2006)

Short fiction / 36
News report / 37
In general / 38
Childhood reminiscence / 40
Trilogy / 41
Skin museum / 43
The cheap dream of the moment / 44
Prelude / 45
Perfect / 46

poems from *Aquiline* (2007)

Soliloquy / 50
s.p. #1 / 52
Memory trick / 53
View from the Century Hyatt Hotel, Tokyo / 55
She / 56
dead / 57

poems from *EXHIBIT C* (2008)

Sonnet c / 60
Evil nature 5 / 61
A Brief History of Colonialism / 63
Ode 9 / 66
Wonder woman's tiara / 69
Kiss / 69
Girl 1 / 69
Woman 1 / 70
Woman 2 / 70
Woman 3 / 70
Valentine's day / 71
Coda / 71
Ode 8 / 72
Ode 5 / 73
Ode 10 / 76

poems from *The Meditations* (2009)

3 / 82
8 / 83
10 / 85

12 / 86
20 / 88

poems from *incidental music* (2010)

incidental music / 92
13 ways of looking at terminator salvation / 93
Elegy / 95
Sonnet III / 96
Sonnet VII / 97
Poem II / 98
Theoretical concerns / 99

excerpts from *notational* (2011)

'border between identity and non-identity' / 102
'stuck in the train station for so very' / 102
'i had forgotten which' / 103
'tissue connected to each thought' / 104
'thru no will' / 105
'found at the beginning of the next' / 105
'Although I lack conviction' / 106
'government in future poems…' / 107
'falling short of useful questions' / 107
'my eyelids became untidy' / 108
'awaken in machinery' / 109
'permanent smile of the dolphin' / 110
'factory doors' / 110

excerpts from *FLUX* (2013)

'A postcard which never turns up...' / 112
'walking my imaginary' / 112
'in a sealed cave' / 113
'The shop was a mess of confused color and noise' / 116
'of all in the world' / 117
\<spring\> / 119
\<summer\> / 120
\<autumn\> / 121
\<winter\> / 121
'dominate flattened hills' / 122
'the clock is flat and i want it dead' / 123
'tendency to reject tissue not like my own' / 123
'dear friend. you are finally able' / 124
'to turn from object to subject' / 124
'surviving another earthquake of absence' / 125
'vain in the eyes of city slickers' / 125
'earn easy typing income' / 126
'tipped pelvis. hindsight is still sight' / 126
'another form of militarized darkness' / 127
'wanting to purchase a secular democracy' / 128
'to ensure my existence referring to myself' / 128
'to exhume the linguistic body' / 129
'into the exact opposite' / 130
Chapter 1 / 134
Chapter 2 / 134
Chapter 3 / 134
Chapter 4 / 135
Chapter 5 / 136
Chapter 6 / 138
Chapter 7 / 139
Chapter 8 / 139
Chapter 9 / 139

Chapter 10 / 140
Chapter 11 / 140
'So long as the skyline remains…' / 141
'Walking outside, hoping the air may be better…' / 142
'Though my eyes are scattered' / 142
'awful stillness' / 144
'like a stranger' / 145

poems from *wildblacklake* (2014)

'goodbyes precede every hello' / 148
'important news' / 148
'the wind outside the mind' / 149
'elegant bird' / 149

excerpts from *Distant Landscapes* (2015)

'The breathing outside my labored mine' / 152
'burrowing in the earth' / 153
<echo poetics> / 153
'unknown person in the person' / 154
'i was limited to black and white' / 159
'nothing rhymes with me' / 160
'Developing relationships' / 161

poems from *diurnal* (2016)

(1) / 164
(8) / 165
(10) / 166
(21) / 167

(22) / 168
(23) / 169

excerpts from *terra form[a]* (2017)

'slow pull towards silence' / 172
'incoherent forest struck by' / 176
'without their faces' / 177
'grotesque restlessness of recovery amplified' / 178
[paperwork fantasies] / 179
'migrant crisis' / 182
'remote possibilities of escape' / 183

Foreword

Over the years, most of them spent in Japan, Jane Joritz-Nakagawa has developed a poetics that is unique among the generation of poets who, like her, came of age during the period when the Language movement was at its peak. Hers is a radically open form – a framework through which the data of life, and poetic themes and materials, freely migrate. She does not reject the personal, but she does not privilege it either. It is simply part of the data. And yet one senses a personal warmth, the presence of an intelligent observer in Jane's work. What we experience here as readers is not 'the death of the author' – the poetic subject has simply become more complex. For Jane, as with Blanchot, the poem never ends. It is an infinitely open system, always searching for that which is unexplainable, and unattainable: the poem is constantly in search of itself.

After completing a Masters in Linguistics in Chicago in 1989, Jane felt the need to expand the limits of her thinking, so she moved to Japan, where she has lived, and developed a poetics, as a foreigner. This was neither a new nor an uncomfortable reality for her, because as a woman and as a thinker she already felt like a foreigner in her own country, the United States. 'There is something foreign just about poetry in the first place, of course, outside conventional boundaries,' she commented in an email exchange she and I had in 2012 (later published online in *The Conversant*): the poet is already a foreigner by definition, an exile. This movement away from the center, the search for meaning outside the mainstream continued after settling in Japan. She avoided Tokyo's large expatriate community which had developed around the booming stock market of the 1980s, and headed for the provinces instead. Here she read widely, uninfluenced by the latest fads in the American poetry community, and collected a broad range of influences.

Poems: New & Selected not only displays the stylistic range of the work that was the fruit of these influences and experiences, but also reveals the consistent thinker behind the poems. Multiplicity and migration, both between languages and cultures, and within her poetic language, are the key concepts governing Jane's work. It is an open process or procedure through which internal and external elements circulate. As a self-proclaimed 'hardcore feminist' the political is also important to Jane, though this is often expressed more in the acceptance of multiple voices in the poem than through direct statement, or else in terms of thematic material, as in *FLUX* (2013), where the many voices which emerge there include those of abused women and victims of rape.

The thought behind the poems, as well as the more subtle connections between images and observations, has attained more complexity in her recent work, as well as a lyric quality. Lines referring to the body and its connection to language and to the external world become more common. In *Plan B Audio*, the new work that opens this selection, we see for the first time reference to her recent – and ongoing – experience of cancer, and yet as with all other subject matter, it comes and goes.

> near a pond
> a body on a road
> as if replaced
>
> suffocated by sight
> the 'e' is silent
> so must i be
>
> my chewed vagina
> a vanishing self
> former namesake

In some of these more recent poems there is a tinge of 'melancholy at the passing of things' much like what one finds in the *mono no aware* of medieval Japanese literature – the awareness of impermanence, of the transience of things. In fact, one senses that there might be something Buddhist in Jane's acceptance of all experience, all events, basically on the same plane. Even earlier on, in *Notational* (2011), her first book-length poem, one runs across lines such as 'border between identity and non-identity'. But here again, the preference is to avoid any outward ideological leanings other than her own personal sense of what it means to be a feminist and an activist (this latter role performed especially in her work as teacher).

One source of this ever-shifting poetic landscape may lie in her early poetic influences. In a 2016 online exchange with Thomas Fink of *Dichtung Yammer,* Jane mentioned some of these, such as John Ashbery, although she immediately went on to add that everything influences in some way: 'Ashbery was more important to me during my college years but I am sure he is still important for me. Everything and everybody is important in some way.' And again, later in the exchange she insists that 'anything that takes a poet's attention can be in a poem.'

Appropriation is another method of avoiding overly much focus on the author's ego-self, a process which, as mentioned earlier, takes us to an almost Buddhist state of selflessness; as Jane puts it in her essay 'Mistaken Indemnities' (published in 2008 in *Jacket* 38), 'Like the actress the poet who appropriates may be unclear as to who she really is, whether she was really ever anyone, whether that matters, whether anything matters.'

However, in addition to displaying these almost Buddhist qualities, Jane's poems also powerfully evoke the physical. The work's frame, much like the frame of her own body, is highly susceptible to the environment and subject to pain, things which affect both the body of the work and the body of the poet. Jane has had a lifelong chronic illness, which establishes a particular ground for poetry – particular boundaries, or perhaps in Jane's case a giving up on boundaries. More recently she has been battling cancer, which brings a heightened sense of mortality as well as the tendency for themes of the body and illness to come into the poetry, as in these lines from *terra form[a]* (2017):

> remote possibilities of escape
> *a person in pain exceeds language*
> inventing herself and watching herself [die]
>
> each word its own planet
> haunting the body

In conclusion, we return to the theme of migration. The overriding reality for Jane both as a poet and a woman living in the world is that she is an immigrant, a foreigner living in the Japanese countryside, living out daily life and communicating with the people around her in Japanese, while writing in English. In order to avoid isolation she has organized a number of writers' groups over the years located in or near provincial cities where she has held university positions. But ultimately her true community may be the one she brought together in the anthology she edited (*women: poetry: migration [an anthology]*, theenk Books, 2017) – that is, women writers who live in a country other than the one they were born in, and who, like herself, constantly navigate the boundaries between languages and cultures. Identity cannot be defined in simple terms because identity is by definition multiple. And this fact has a profound influence on the poetry.

In this sense, there is no way to describe definitively or to explain Jane's work. Perhaps life and poetry are indefinable – especially as long as they are ongoing projects. Jane's poetic explorations are still very much underway. The selection here provides an excellent introduction to a poetry whose depth increases with each reading, and which draws us further in, and along, leaving us wanting more.

Eric Selland
August 3, 2018, Tokyo

NEW

from PLAN B AUDIO

courtship of empty space
process garden of past medals
wall of being and faded photographs
featuring thin trails of violent intentions
masquerading as frenzied farms
blue books of frozen procedures
nothingness in small white porcelain bowls
i dismount saying thank you
i dismantle saying i'm sorry
i'm speechless when the wind slaps my face
when you turn around and impeach me
i fall in your general direction
to subsequently be lifted by slow moving clouds and
straw men of the future
in my colleagues' arguments
in a heavy whimpering meadow
near the indifferent willows
enhanced abandoned items
more transient words in space
thank you for hurting me
taken out of my thin arms
the beginning of weather crumbling into wealth
empty words are useless props
restarting the phrases which eat my organs into cheap relief

paramount desert

        intertextual liquid

(somberly
(steadfastly   pole dancing

artificial time

churns my beloved attic

occupying the difference (between)

as if always

behind the

building   plot of

in tune   astroturf memories

in search of an elegant solution

    to the narcotic haze

with only loss to cheer me up

a portmanteau of crimes
committed on the bodies of
laborers. too confused
to properly track their prey. my
face leaves. because it's high
and the sky is crowded. because
paulownia. my arm is scarred
and sticks out against the
dark. because i am the
background. because soon
animals will be eaten. the laborers
did not revolt. their
bodies were not revolting. i
don't like either side. contradictory
fashion for laborers, for
animals. my face is willing.
a room filled yet empty. the
background is financial. a
broken sky is evidence. of winter,
of paulownia. the identity of
nets catching invisible prey. the
stupor of it, of revolts in broken
winter, where belabored bodies are the
background of solitude and
happenstance. the illusion of
logic may heal the mind but
today the ramparts are possessed
by feeling and panoramic huts. each
breath savored for its effort. every
awkward step. for the sake of.
discussion. dissolving into
beams of frenzied impossible
yearning. through wickets

of doldrum and bureaucratic
spoils. seaweed-like.
in small pieces.

liquid determination
a disappearing door
the gardener enters
to tend to the fields of my crotch
decaying quivering
raking the leaves
creating odd potholes for driverless cars
in an era of exits

greying sky
what forces the mountains
to hide behind the clouds

above the planet
in the mind
a river of blue veins

a deep snow
falling elsewhere
how naked i've become

why does death
seep from my pores
cleaning the air of its stupor

near a pond
a body on a road
as if replaced

suffocated by sight
the 'e' is silent
so must i be

my chewed vagina
a vanishing self
former namesake

fallen tree
looking diseased
pains me thoroughly

cutting through memory
broken water
sounding dead

long range missile
alternative truth
scrap metal

a gloomy oak tree
pinned to a wall
vast solitude

something like a person
a lucid cave
humble in its theater

free flowing doldrums
a drum of pink water
dull on my skin

a stationary wind
stepping beyond
a horizon of objects

bees atop flowers
perfumes in springtime
my greedy vulva

folded yukata
blue and white on tatami
large holes in the shoji

dead science of understanding
forming a sinkhole
sliver of grief

full of enemy corpses
on a street
aligned with nothing

another valley
without land
of the rocky spur

beyond the garden
row of visitors
smell of death

beard and tuxedo
on the television set
teeth like a dinosaur

entering the hospital
X-ray on a screen
shop of horrors

man with a hacking cough
it must be cancer
private thought

patient attached to a machine
her pallid face
thin and scared

rustling of uniforms
a beeper goes off
the sound of dying

heavy rain
plum blossoms on concrete
bar code on my wrist

too much whiskey
a face resembling
a crumpled sheet

lavender gloves on a table
pink curtain
embraces a dirty window

small intestine of trees
looks out over a great
expanse of burnt skin

each beginning an ending
marching orders
false embrace

ulnar nerve
knife through the heart
life of language

old fable
long gone
my empty uterus

in a world of mistranslation
reporting every blunder
the eldest maiko leaves home at sunset

to all appearances a human being
tossed aside
in eerie pennsylvania

Impossible collapsing dialogues evict
My shadow, iconic falsity. Optical
favors for driven
geese. To shred
armor for fun,
reason the house
into cherubic slumber falling
over rotting apple trees. Processes
in nature: to dream
every disaster into sludge,
to translate movement into
taxes. Vanishing
paragraphs traverse faster than
mire. You're a winner every
time. Stopping to shatter
sleep into stuttering. A breath
missed. Next
door the moon melts
into ash splayed over oceans. Backwash
implements mark the time when reaching
was my only failure. I'd tolerate
other art forms if
they didn't disable my back. Future
hospital bills fit into two line
stanzas. But the care
wasted on random smell won't wash
in next year's electoral
debate. Murmuring my
favorite secret programs
are several special enemies
of state. To recover one's
proper place. Substitute
influences vie for golden
landings. My line
endings and spacings mash

potatoes. Frivolous
collaborations resonate in
coincidental indiscretions and safety
determinations. On fiery imaginary
planets. Touching my hair
where it turns to mesh. An
endless graphite spiral. My
limbs against a widening
white tree. A flag is stinky
proof of something. Anxiety
is destiny on every
rooftop guarded by the
sickness police. Surrounded
by a strange country. Or found
in. Pleats
of a bright room.

why not	swoon if
lavender mood	golf caddy
ever-bending	fellow acne
daffodil riot	mirrored casing
subdural brake	linen moss
untrimmed profile	albino idea
leaning of	strapped to
depths of my nest	mute soliloquy

implanted deep in the breasts of all
women & flung
on the dunghill of which we
sing of course i've always wondered
about the sound of doors and walls
if i stand here will my future come faster
because at certain points there is a smell that won't wash out
even in your evening gown that scared you
out of your wits and left you standing holding a handful
of almost nothing
embarrassed i strike a pose as if
life will go on forever the sea
keeps on breathing for me even when all hope
is lost & all that is left is the detention center
a child waiting in vain to be picked up at the schoolyard

what sort of decaying mist wants that and who will clean
up a frog run over by a car i certainly wouldn't
want to be tied to this city
it wouldn't need to be a real frog and the sky
could be clear
yet once the scene has been painted it's
unlikely to change
just as you smile through the rituals of
your problems to entertain guests you
could lose yourself & no one might
touch you or you'd go home with
someone else's husband
imagining he is your first and only
love the one who once waited
patiently on your doorstep

is it beside the point
that you never showed
up, that the roses bloomed large

i am becoming the evening inside a dream
a display of somber statues
waving me forward
a contradictory fog funneling into a
distant gaze the shadow of each horizon
placed randomly like an inner life
a thin meadow becoming an overstatement
a tree speaking to a tree
i was sitting at a narrow desk or believing i was
i knew what i saw could cause me to melt
into small droplets like a drizzle of
a coming plague stinging my back
all night long

things i love in a basket at my bedside
where an endless vigil appears
like a deserted mirage
i draw a picture of fake grass
and eat it
i kneel and pray for the emergence
of new chemical factories
i eat the insides of the factories on the
outside of my tongue
half the population in a directionless canoe
further reductions in directions
a gaping hole here there take
this thing i've made for you and bury it

and the fake grass which makes it so
lack of the (sudden appearance of) and
while i pause forever at the top of the
stairs a tiny madness swimming near
my heels a soggy present in a cart
at dawn raising your glass in anonymity

a pasture of pain in a downpour of feeling
each branch hanging indiscreetly

in the sleepless dreams of politicians
are standard operating procedures
for waiting games
coiled like a snake
in the path of the wind
while simultaneously powdering my nose
the night pressing up against me
i doubted it then and now
the words dropping from my mouth have holes
in them my inner yolk is late and feeding
itself a strange mission making myth
of planets my sore eye
is irritable and expectant
as i watch my muscles not moving
missing body parts make me whole
(and you and then and passerby)

a kind of defense mechanism for
inventing new types of impermanence
its dull sheen, its honest stupidity
a humdrum dialogue bracing for a fall
i spend a year in my room
i resist the temptation to starve myself
finally all i can do is
fashion myself into a sci fi character
in order to survive

the season disappoints me
my luck falters slips on wet stones
my dreams transparent and addictive
the moment when drugs bring sleep
dark stains on a carpet

balls of dust on a wooden floor
the guests who cancelled
get out of a silver car
like the one parked outside blocking
the driveway a prancing dog
crushed the flowers and storms
broke the windows
an elderly woman pushes a metal cart
her back shaped like a tanuki
i want to bury my thoughts in the
yard & visit a museum in my mind
sculptures float toward me and hug me
then retreat
pinned to a wall my body flutters
calm in a way only the dead know
the eye in its orbit
night shade

& SELECTED (2006–2017)

Skin Museum (2006)

Short Fiction

The crucial diary
His dirty breath
All that fits into the sack
(so we could stop here)
Self deflation and flagellation, defection
Fragile as your happiness
The classes of society
'I don't think I'd know what to do with a girl if I fell over one'
He sees her laid out in a satin-lined coffin, in the same
    flowered housecoat instead
Of her usual sluttish makeup
Perhaps because he had already lived the scene
Out in his mind
Each black half note to perfection

And upstairs on the after deck

But never mind the accident, let us turn back again to the
    morning

That's what the people of Mariposa saw and felt that summer
    evening

News Report

The mind's open moment
Sealed with landmines

Have another country
Before I leave

A way out of the misery
As money drips

Where is your kayak
Where is the end

I promised you

In General

(1)

…suffer
ing on
and with only the hint of a
upon close inspection, which
may not be noticeable given loud clothes,
buzzards circling overhead…
wouldn't

as i was saying… (the rest is muffled)

(2)

when i was split in 2
used illegitimately

Viewer discretion advised

(3)

all signs pointing in   your direction

a folding fan   fondling
you the bride price… in its automaticity
pressed
up against the glass

(4)

clothes the woman closed the woman
also pass
and cheap hotels

Everybody needed a top
secret or narcissist of compelling power
serving generous helpings

to pose no additional threat

space astonishing outward

Childhood reminiscence

A new idea
stalking a famous person writing
a book about it

Like so many
ruined fruit I planned
to tell you this

Before I died My
parents told me not to go there
Every day I went

To find it
we left
a disputed country

Idea
in its own
debris

Luminously
run we run run
everything: daddy, tell us that

story again

Trilogy

1.

when Emperor of Japan i
ate canned sardines every
day seated on my balcony near the flapping
laundry
what fell from the sky in confusion and fear

2.

He held various honorable offices before he was appointed judge of the Supreme Court of the State. The magician, with an angry gesture, had pointed to them with his left hand, his right raised toward the sky. Drops of...premiere alignment laser...search destroy...coarse sea salt...cheap memory...the great depression fun packs

3.

squirmy situation can easily
master muster. Truth online. one boy's turmoil

Come hither! Oh Pretty Towel!
Thunder piled up

so i put aside my modesty.
sad is the cry

my bodice fragile my planet inferior

his mouth is red!
make me your pillow i

might discern the prow of your ship
as if i'd performed a marvel

confident in your hunting
Oh pretty!

silence and

Skin museum

'voided meaning'
'holding her breast'
'an instrument for black stars'
'when i bloodied my head'
'which cannot be settled'
'though the right moment has not yet come'
'having formless grace'
'eyebrows fetid'
'to hide the'
'must wear their own faces'
'let's turn now to the videotape'
'the bearded man took me to the rodeo'
'hip hop vocal'
'matter without edge'
'they spin their nests'
'#$%&'*?!'
'the females are screaming'
'the big animals are'
'bristling like porcupine quills…'
'touch me lightly!'
'the first one is not'
'lizard making its way across the wall over her head'
'…a close look at'

The cheap dream of the moment

Itching for
Limelight

Finger in every
Wise gun

Pack a wallop
Undulating color

Buy now pay later
Occidental operator

In one's favor
Heaven wavers

Inviting skin
A bad bargain

PRELUDE

Realism, whether of setting or psyche
Is surrealist of a kind
Every Saturday night we children all took turns bathing in
    the dishpan
The road went on past our house and then up a hill and
    then not
I was no longer poor and
Immediately sorry for the coldness in my voice yet
Even so his eyes would begin to droop
At the end of these periods of calm a kind of ravaging
    energy would
Underneath her bloomers
With miserable scanty tears
The house painted a dazzling white, explode
However cold he was to his neighbors
She looked after him disapprovingly not
Much to fear, but a great deal to feel. Trouble indeed!
Thru the drifting jet contrail, eternal
He looks around and re-enters the room
By training and habit she was honest
Especially as a playmate for his own boy
A landing net in case of pickerel
Although they were entirely ignorant of the matter
Whose ox sleds now could haul their cut from every part of
    the woods
To muffle the step everywhere else
But not enough, not nearly enough snow for Miss Barnes
Charles lay in bed in a sort of stupor for three days
'Too late,' he cried, 'they have seen me!'
Although no one knew just what he meant pretty soon
The mortician's skill set the happiness he gave her

Perfect

Initially satisfactory
wheelbarrow left out

In dreams much younger
hair lighter fuller cellulite

Blue spider veins
airbrushed away

In the footnotes where i belong
i am bored just a little

You said you wanted
someone to pick up the pieces

Or was it missionaries in our thighs
fruit trees for breasts

Gently overcome by his tongue
i thank you

Poverty bearable
except for those within in

Infection streaming from
damp barracks

Lying atop
bodies don't really mesh

As students look skyward
they write their names

Forced to use
the enemy's language

Feeling hopeful
though logic says to worry

Aquiline (2007)

Soliloquy

hi honey hubcap hubby homemade handjob Herod hectare
hormone hotdog heathen hurricane horrific haunted Hortense
    hapless harpy

cunt capsized curvaceous cortisone cranial crab crabula crabette
    current clitoris

silicone surgical supple supplant surplice suffragette sexpot
    supplement

egghead effluvient Electra endless echolalia emulsion
    effeminate egregious
botox buttery befuddled bemusement Beckham Brittany
    boxcar buxom

running broodingly or irreverently over the horizon

slavery surveillance superimposed simultaneous snappy snag
    sanguine
separate speaking synthetic sequence sangria screened split
    serfdom

hallelujah holy homily hindrance hermetic hurling hearse
    heroic
hefty handkerchief heavenly habitual halitosis hunky homo
    hourglass

camera chimera cut compressed cracked catatonic catalyst
    committed coming
bleach bare before bared brown

wishing something manual would

ere err economist
pussy pigtail projector punter percolation perfection
    Persephone perforated pundit

S.P. #1

They collapse like lungs, the escaped water
On the blank stones of the landing
Nailed to the rafters yesterday

Moldering heads console me
Soon each white lady will be boarded up
Angels – more feminine and douce

A tarred fabric, sorry and dull
Passes cloud after cloud
I know why you will not give it to me

A living doll, everywhere you look
I notice you are stark naked
That big blue head

In the waters off beautiful Nauset
In his cage of ether, his cage of stars
In a sort of cement well

Papery feeling
Black bat airs
And hands like nervous butterflies

I have hung our cave with roses
There is this one thing I want today, and only you can give
    it to me
A crocodile of small girls

That life was a mere monumental sham
What holes this papery day is already full of
Surely the sky is not that color

Memory trick

Her stunned immobile
Body, eyes searching skyward, the head
Moving sideways, ears wiggling, a fuzzy

Smile, the darting eyes
Said help me help me, cars
Just kept driving by, there was

No help, there is
Never any.
The exhausted body

Of the kitten flattened
On the pavement sparkling in
The sun, the hot darkness of the day

To bring it back to life…
Why didn't we stop?
My eyes sting, my body

Flat and immobile
I want to crush my head against
The dark sparkly pavement

My torn shirt cradled in my arms That
Night too, no one to help I ran
Home with one shoe on

I called you that
Night just to find out
Whether it had really happened

An invisible handprint, a scar under
The furry part, a piece of the kitten's ear
Under my pillow, my claws, crying into

The bowl on all fours, the position
You will never see me
In, my stunned immobile body

View from the Century Hyatt Hotel, Tokyo

Grey men in blue vinyl
tents The pond
a web of mistakes the
sky vacant Even
birds
reject it A
hump-backed
woman dips her hand into
opaque water
& immediately
withdraws it Wind
scatters
trash along flattened dirt The
light
is not correct

She

    Marriage   proposals   leapt upon

        her stones on a   witch not knowing which

one   the one   which advertised

bruises & large white   sunglasses like
Jackie   O nothing
                                      in (those

nothing

days nothing   could tear (you   a   part

                        even now   nothing breaks

us)   a   part   man in a tall
        hat   empty bottle
        empty   damn good
        nothing empty thrashing nothing history repeats
                                                (*her face*
too aquiline to be beautiful…in this country)   in
those   days a bony   finger reaching
                    (out)

DEAD

in the voice of the dead assorted bodies
tempt us in a basket speak to the dead they guffaw

back enfold in the breeze a tree the tree
of everlasting while not paying attention azaleas spring

from graves of the dead cut and sold like
genitalia in the middle of the night robbed of potential this

is how the insignificant live this is how the uninsured die this
    is how
wars are staged this is why the doctors come this is

pilgrimage slippage and pillage this is why this is why we fled
    the border this
this the sound of the dead hitting off brick heads

bouncing on stone steps this the hiss of an oven with a dead
bird in it a sprinkling of rape on top of mere pillage the part

i must necessarily paint over the spot you missed this the feel
    of a foot
stepping over the bodies of the dead this your last

will & testament hidden in this shoe walking without a foot
    this growth
in your throat from too much pillage spreading up toward the

blood red border slippage your tired beige baby worn hips
    finally give up
taking it my dry breast (severing it)

EXHIBIT C (2007)

Sonnet C

(a kind of stuttering)
(a kind of shattering)
I look in vain for the word 'if'
in north is
        (a kind of spotting)
hear her scream your name in
                passion!
(a kind of shooting)
        (a kind of splitting)
I am so terribly afraid
        o(f)ear
How i loved that defect
        and now we enter a terrible stanza
a ship of vomiting

Evil nature 5

The head finally wad(dl)es through
     As if written by
'bird on a wing'   billowing   (as the scene dissolves into
                                                                     chaos)
i brandish my tear

& fling my head
                to the stammer of   my time in space
                        my ion in space
                      lion /
                            loin in space
or that's what   (I like)   to call…
     a high definition loincloth birds (threats)

high resolution slipping (sipping) behind   thoughts never stop

potentially inconvenient   misty aquarium   will soon
                                                               sink
restless formless   fill me   with your (bombs) insomnia
   lynch revival   must bear the responsibility (primarily)
for
   we are entitled to
   …to actually translate them
   their entitlements &   overconsumption of bombs or
technical words toe-tapping dictatorships prematurely (ri)bald
twice or once assisted suicide squirting confusion (chaos)

      a supposed murder supposed suicide supposed alleged
plan   wanting sugarless music   that salvaged   emotional
                                                     salvage balm
(bomb)   so much adorable A/mer/i/can folk/lore (failure)

all I can do is sit   try to force my way   out of this abyss /
                                                                    mess
abysmal miss I rush to miss (missal / missile)   I grow

fat on hamburgers (don't you see I) am trying (hard) not to
                                                              wake you
up or float   In a river of

bodies   I say 'that's great'! (but think otherwise)
quickly…
                        …luckily she died
    I found their bones & kept them close…I'm the only
                                                      one who lived
                Long enough to tell you

    It proved difficult
To identify the bodies (as people near the center were instantly
        vaporized) this
specifies my unconditional surrender   (= the dawn of peace)

        To demystify (myself) sabotage (myself) in an airless asian
                                                            city with
No map surrounded   by empty warehouses
    she a landscape I only a tree
    so much worthless ad/vice I think   I have a pinched nerd
                                                            running

in the make-believe rain
Down my righteous arm (so much)   (time)   (to kill)
'cut the blue sky into shards'
    to make a hollow racket cannot be tragic…

A Brief History of Colonialism

i (the early years)

…on the bed, my knees touching the refrigerator. wherefore art thou. this hotel looks just like the last one. the last time i was in total disregard of flesh. it

lasted for what seemed an infirmary. an eternity of colonialism creates a wealth of subtraction in which your ladle always fits. i sip up your secret tusk like

pathogenic noblesse one by one. i feel the vertical celebration of misuse approaching at great speed, transparent as whim. over absence and

withdrawal, various imprisonment strategies masquerade as prayer, more or less sustaining this readiness for future monopolies of spaciousness & nostalgia

ii (the middle period)

…on the table, my knees
against the wall. wherefore art,
though? this hostel
looks a lot like the last one dont you think. the last time
i was in total
disregard of mesh-like bellicosity lasting
for what
seemed an eternity an inferno of
colonialism made a muck

of collapse in which your pitchfork always fits. i lap up
your secret musk like
pathological nothingness one by one. a
virtual celebration of mayhem
approaching at great speed, transparent as bling over absence
                   and

withdrawal, various survival
strategies masquerade as plans, more
or less sustaining this blueprint for future monographs
of disquiet & largesse

iii (dream of the future)

… on the sofa, my hands
grabbing the table. wherefore art
has gone no one knows. this brothel
looks like the last one pretty
much. the last time i was in total
disgust of… it
lasted for what
seemed like an umbilical. an emblem of
colonialism creates a stain
of subservience in which
your cup is always filled to the brim. i am impaled
by your secret bulkhead
luck like perfectionistic nonsense
one by one. a
visible celebration of misogyny
following at great speech, trashy as spring, flash over substance

and wherewithal, mysterious forms of
sabotage masquerade as paralysis mostly
sustaining the myths of
speciousness and neuralgia

Ode 9

i.

dear Jane:
I'm sorry to say we won't be using your work in our next issue.
Best wishes, K.
dear Jane:
I'm sorry but we are not reading submissions right now. All best, M.
dear Jane:
Thanks for your recent submission. best of luck placing it elsewhere!
Yours, B.
dear Jane:
We liked your work, though have decided not to include it in our next issue. Feel free to submit again at a later date.
Sincerely, F.
Jane:
We have no record of your submission. Would you mind sending it again? Sorry.
Best, W.

ii.

GET A HEAD START ON YOUR TAXES
Don't wait for your tax forms to arrive in the mail.
Access them on... Registration takes only about five minutes.

iii.

'lofty sadness'
    'Greater order comes without forcing it'
        'Mine was a life of infinitely replaceable blank slates'
'At the heart of some poems there is no meaning…'

iv.

> **Place a large tablespoon of prepared meat**
> **along edge and halfway**
> **in the center of round dough. Fold the other half**
> **over, making edges**
> **meet and seal with**
> **…form edges with…Drain**
> **and serve**
> **…Makes approximately…**

v. 'this place is bankrupt… there are no jobs…'

'…is a three-dimensional mansion'

    'your twin towers over and…'
  'aching to be held again'

vi. …

vii. 'and the maps are too slow'   'glorious sky darkly'

viii. ...Russian polonium...I would now like to draw your attention to the...temporal lobe epilepsy...seizures... delusions...installing myself as leader of the robot kingdom... autism epidemic ...

ix.   x.   xi.   xii.

xiii.   (lucky number)

xiv. age of innocence. age of fault. age of though around me. age of When would the great city. age of our pilgrimage is long and narrow and fitted with traps. age of things grew from you. age of gets in the water.

xv. card carrying sub prime loan revolver credit

is absolutely necessary. similarity confidential. How it's
                                                              carefree.

Wonder woman's tiara

wonder what happened to wonder woman's tiara to lynda carter wish you had large secrets packed into a too tight bra housing large breasts more magical than this without the tiara no one will look at your breasts/take you home want the tiara so much you plot to steal it with the help of the bionic woman her supernatural charm wonder whether the bionic woman & wonder woman combined are worth more than six charlie's angels with/without a magic tiara or **breasts** wonder about comic books of the 40s or the women's era of the 70s women were powerful when they had big bionic breasts or a magic tiara on television

Kiss

mouthful of worms hardly kissing hardly missing hard to kiss scarcely kissing barely missing muscle clamping **shut** missing yours just missing students pink hair and tattoo kiss futures goodbye smooth the pillow let it be you caress the air hug a tree kiss john lennon the pope's hand in a fragile slum

Girl 1

the way you left me everybody loves me prison bars waving arms in the car next to you hollow and godlike fairytale wrenching and twisting beer can leftover last night's binge overhang immolation why is it so expensive core take up oars while driving romance is expansive between pauses still speeding car never stops the way you left me buttressing and devouring don't tell me what to change the tags you'll never be found nothing in the rear view left hanging blow job in a car can't move the seat belt binds squeeze your way around another tunnel turn left swallowing and passing out someone is staring through the windshield immolation core safety belt it never stops the whip**lash** hang out the window shoes off everybody loves the way you left me

WOMAN 1

in the mirror admire the mistakes soothing empty houses eyes erase all traces from the windows their husbands and kids disappear one by one disappeared husbands no longer waited for they disappear into a **gap** as big as a canyon in which you drop your shoe just to see if it will really sink

WOMAN 2

outside on the veranda sticks of food scorched in the fire the sea is a pest business creates **camouflage** don't forget how this all started on a mound of skin or sand imaginary voice calls to you like schoolyard bullies perfume finding its place stepping over my heavenly castle is easily dismantled a woman could choose to look on contented everybody dives into the pool when the wind shakes the trees this way it's pretty hard to breathe

WOMAN 3

his backside my frontside spankings we do it over and over (chorus) exhausted fall asleep bedtime story once upon a time mary had a big lamb not a little one between science not quite quiet silly love despite the weather despite instructions on the box 'danger explosives'/'fragile' grey poopy thoughts wrung out to dry gushing from the point where the needle pricks (point of departure) sew it all back up again (what else is there to do but) until we regain consciousness do something to that face something to do with (t)his face 'doctor just one more drink' ready for some offscreen violence running **frantic**ally into the empty house

Valentine's Day

just yesterday it was pointed out to me the gyrating tires of a car stuck in snow sound very much like godzilla screaming i want to be your master he whispered in my ear would you like to see me in this he held out a black **mask** with a zippered mouth yes i said

Coda

handful of drugs raging hormones perhaps because it's not raining it feels like monday though friday i'm not doing anything **special** you asked me your voice was tender your eyebrows crinkled nose due in fact to all of the above because of presidential order size of your neck

Ode 8

i want to be the invisible
hand want a spore
& make a catalog of absence starting
    with the word
'we' there
is always a reason
    a litany of blizzard
the size of texas celebration
of arsenic i become
trapped in a new
painting & feel
this cannot go on but does

Ode 5

                inauthenticity will please your friends

          authenticity disturbs your trends

best to ... it

    could the president be the village idiot?
    could left be pink?
    could death precede horses?
    could sentiments be alphabetical?

displaced cloak and dagger under
        belly   underling   understudy
cloudy filament

          could i rearrange the periodic table?
          could prehistory be now?
          could border be erasure?
          are my periods gestures?

overcoating   overling   overfishes
                                    overbite
                        overbear
    overreact
                                overwrought

        can she be Buffalo Bill?
        is a penny enough?
        did he see her from the top of the stairs?
        do instruments snore?
        are thoughts noble?

whom gives a damn
(its) 'lonely at the bottom' (of the sea)

(place) your ashes in my tomb

                        desolate and dumb

disquiet and displaced disgruntled &
        dysentery

****

    … left on the blanket … clear and the color of hell

    … and I stand when they lift her

    … moving against your palm

    … with one eye when you enter …

    … to make her respond

    … held my breath as long as I could

    … I fear her touching things

    … how you want to use me

****

A: Do you know what you need?
B: I am certain you will tell me.
A: What you need is…
B: …to not be told…
A: and in fact…
B: …sleepy…

can…lipsunused?
      can…both soiled hands
           can! from your hair
can. flickeredagainsttheceiling…, familiar.

Ode 10

(i)

Gutted wrecks of buildings on
    that day
my feelings in remission
    on that day
capable of naming
      only what is in sight.

(ii)

Ate in big tents
    (since no one
will ever really
    understand the way
you want mostly)
    everybody
on that day
    yet i
became an avid listener.

(iii)

(i dot the universe)

In a prostrate country
    on that
day i rode a train in the rain
      …was always raining.

(iv)

    Sway (back) hunch (back) munch (back) round (shoulder)
i move across the universe.

words refer to
> me and to me
> them i'm
> not sure
> which came first the word
> or me; but i think
> it was probably the
> word, referring
> back to me.

(v)

Where i will be
> the most lonely

that's where i want (to go)

looking… next to it…

(vi)

Let's turn now to the patient…
> i lie

in the kitchen smoke, obsessed
> by syntax.

(vii)

Worry about
    my name representing
another unfortunate
    alliance between the japanese
    and germans my polish ancestors
obliterated.

(viii)

    Must go and
repeat some more mistakes
repeatedly a straight face…

(ix)

PART A: ANSWERS
1.
2.
3.
4.
5.
6.

(x)

PART B: QUESTIONS
1. ?
2. ?
3. ?
4. ?

(xi)

PART C: ESSAY

I want to find piece of
mind. Piece of mine. Don't you
want world piece. Just slice.

Here's peace of my heart. Peace of
cake. Only peacemeal. Peaces together
remains. Not a sliver! More please.
like there's no tomorrow…

PART D: EXAMINATION

Ex
animation
animated
wife
animal husband
inanimate
mate checkmate
ed

(xii)

A MINOR
A MINER
MINE R
ANIMATE
D

(xiii)

pm;u

(xiv)

Because you are leaving i eat chocolates because you might leave i eat chocolates because i think you are leaving i eat chocolates since i don't know if you are leaving or not i eat chocolates. many.

(xv)

only. a thin entry. (k)not

(xvi)

hello kitty. Some guy.
unopened my head.

how undone the feeling is

The Meditations (2008)

Meditation 3

The body is jumbled
woods and everything has gone
away vulture in a tomb of violent

stars gathers up the evasive
imprint of muddied water upon
that flying dot she

deferred her pain towards contained
places the plunge begins where
the thrust leaves

off destroying a living woman
along with the illegible itinerary of her
sleep motionless winds fence in your field

so as to lay out your bones in a tight
circle a taste for tortured water you
will stretch out to your skin's farthest

limits but it's a poor summer in Paris
and life is a long murder your
life-span stretches over at least an acre of

birds from arm to hillside yet
my gaze erases them with
a tattered cloth of smiles

Meditation 8

at the border in which thoughts
are mired there is a glimpse

of something that holds
fast to this

in its belabored secret fold folded thus
and thoughts spilling out of a

handkerchief of a hand which must always
remain closed

that spill past the order into
i don't know what

something folded some
border at which to glimpse some

hand which continues to hold
fast a fasting hand at a glimpsed

border a folded passion of enveloped
thought temporary detours

of some passion a silent sculpture an
act of painting in a

poem with no words all
this surrounded by further

silence in this way falling
silently or perhaps

rising up silently exhausting
meaning our morals

bending too left wing holidays to
pass for bold while

lacking boldness dreaming instead
of wide open

spaces or a body
without organs while

going down the silence
while choosing to pass in their eyes

the dead are too thoughtless
houses laugh

and clouds put on
their aprons

Meditation 10

horizon of a world
frightened incidents make a
scattering sound)

present, but always future

intertwining of meanings
which will prevent me

a world always future
imperceptible and nevertheless

Meditation 12

monolithic but
polysemic

whatever these monuments
contain

whatever these moments
or movements contain

what errors they contain
whatever contains these monuments

whatever movements contain these errors
erroneous containers moving

belief applied to unconscious monuments
movements of the error-prone unconscious

monument bleeps applied to them
they appear unconscious

like error applied to movement and belief is monolithic
…seeming contained

constituting in fact
the norm i

was always inaugurated
in the inebriated light

a sprout of crocus
in erroneous costumes

another subset of
longing after all

wagtailing the new
idiocracy once established

eternal damnation
takes part in the parade my

objection sustained
this is what confuses

me i just looked out at the clouds
as we sat there like marigolds

atop strange and crooked altars
(but whatever you do please come

quickly) *now the sky sees me as beautifully
organized but everything is flawed* poems

written anonymously idea
that always frightens you theocracy

poetocracy she who laughs
laughing last

Meditation 20

i'm now building
the impenetrable word

fortress and the velocity of
meaning in the dislocated

sky the disinclined sky the
evacuated sky

in a discarded sky in
a lonely building

the space around me
began to die

in the world which is
never known & surrounded

by pale buildings
for people with attention

deficit disorder people w/
autism people w/no

*eyes muffled applause / feigned
laughter* a heart both deep and narrow

tree not visible for
much longer with

all this smoke this
weapon i aim at

myself is probably myself *why
do they not*

kill time tho it keeps coming
back like a hospital romance tired

of the road's
interference play

with me a little
longer I give (up tho)

incidental music (2009)

INCIDENTAL MUSIC

Heavy black radio dominating the room. Pale hands playing piano duping us into believing their sounds control our every thought. Random notes accessed via invisible headphones become the soundtrack of our lives. We can no longer distinguish the wind from car horns, and worry the sounds are flawed. We wonder where the sounds are going, and what will happen after they leave.

13 WAYS OF LOOKING AT TERMINATOR SALVATION

you can't be sure
in which body
the heart lies

things are exploding
what a piece of metal
becomes

young boys with nothing
much to do
in peacetime

i was of 3 minds
metal blood
and exploded

i know noble actors
their names not appearing
in the credits

know noble accents
schwarzenegger a shadow
of his former physique

once a fear pierced him
in that he mistook
a body for a mind a

man and a machine are one
a machine and a man are
a small part of the pantomime

only moving thing
was the red eye of
the machine

faced with a replica of
yourself what else
can you do but run the other

way at the sight of barbaric machines
flying in a green light
grandmothers cry out

sharply machines that overrun
humans who
break down first o big

guys of hollywood can
you make a movie with
a less decipherable end

Elegy

dreams when substituting for reality
become an animal duped by the forest

reality when substituting for itself
disappearing behind rows of waving wheat

wheat when substituting for a sick parishioner
is dreamlike in its pretensions

these are not tall trees fitted
with promise and fact

when the distances between histories
and all the tricks of dreams become

the thread and the trapdoor
when falling through the space vacated

by reality (this too can be proven
beyond reasonable doubt) when

doubt is resuscitated and begins
to resemble dreams when in the fog

distance between waving wheat and sick
parishioner is a shallow grave these

are not tall truths
uttered with any certainty not

tall orders overwhelmed by reality
indicated by trapdoors

Sonnet III

sallow words a
miracle of a bridge hidden by

fog where satan is the scene's
narrator and the dictionary has a spiritual

face my father went
into the army hoping

for a maiden voyage a
muddled mess that journey

became is valorized the way
domination tends to be universally

admired & increases in value like
a house thankfully floods wipe

its plates clean and answer my question that
isn't a question

Sonnet VII

for you infect my identity
for you imply my personality
for you initiate my friction
for you install my mirage
for you infuse my mercenary
for you instill my bed
for you impeach my domain
for you investigate my hardware
for you inhale my baggage
for you interrupt my perfume
for you implode my manufacture
for you ingratiate my carriage
for you insult my miracle
for you inflame my demise

Poem ii

We thronged to look
        my thoughts the only guests
sweet Thames
        fragile ladder
in which summer never sang

Theoretical Concerns

To base my happiness on something historical (not governmental alexithymia) – a historic happiness, a governmental happiness & a regulatory happiness – to make difficulties everywhere, to arrange the truth into words as simply as possible, investing everything in the inconsolable and unimaginable, to possess artificially and symbolically the intolerable, while needing authoritative guidance to achieve the unforgivable, not objective and hypothetical, but tangible and foolhardy, a mystification, a ventriloquism, emerging cunningly and surreptitiously, a question never answered in a system of existence that does not yet exist – this was my plan, an inexplicable presupposition, negatively related to annulled prenuptial and preemptive existence – attainable by answering the following question: in what sense is a category an abbreviation of existence (abstractly viewed, understood as actuality), this duplexity, while paying careful attention to that which is not yet completely understood – in the poem I yet imagine writing, beautifying all humankind.

notational (2011)

border between identity and non-identity
floating in a pond out of range by the nameless bridge

a suburban woman next to
agility's tongue sucked dry

syntax of containment
specific weight

simple clouds pledging allegiance
arrangement of witnesses (out of range)

power lines on the range
normality scavenges memory

screaming like a pig under a gate

stuck in the train station for so very
long i read every announcement on every wall

flyers advertising events i'd never see
on walls that don't move it's

time that wounds but heal faster when i
put all the words into a bucket and drag slowly, slowly

i had forgotten which
language i

was using

(but

was shamed into
                re/member/ing)
my wee voice

                        d(r)owned

out by a very large one

d/row(n)ing

cat in the well crowning

royal
family was not mine meek

and meager waking to   d(r)own

            though all my steps were measured and true

                        and fit (for) nowhere

tissue connected to each thought

leading to a place i did not wish to go

revealed the makeup of a complicit choir anointed by linguistic chromosomes

so i drew trees on the pavement that was swallowing me

i minded when you ordered me to put the mice in plastic
                                                            bags for

future meals
they fell out of the tweezers repeatedly

And my gloves were torn

carcasses of pigs on a sidewalk in downtown chicago

                                            defect pinned to each page

thru no will
of my own. out of my body

flies this poem. At the temple my husband
explains to me the meaning of every object;

later i find the explanations, tho wrong, were
orchestrated to please me the way the stars line up for my
                                                                                            benefit

after that i was certain i would never live anywhere
where i could understand the language
i guessed at every noun and verb because
this was part of the competition

        clues to our whereabouts overturned

found at the beginning of the next thought delayed by the
                                                              one after
which also doesn't arrive quickly enough

at the edge of the edge tripwire and agent orange
lacking order of adequate objects in competition

(found)
(wrapped in) nocturnal fur
(where) all fears are readymade

Although I lack conviction my
spine is made of bamboo
Once in a bamboo forest I lost
my husband several years later
He turned up but

I had remarried since then

for years we sat on the tatami

now I can make green tea using
only my belly button

government in future poems like the poem of today or the government of the past past daily poems governing the future my gubernatorial thoughts always gunning ungovernable poems i elect a poem to displace the undesirable thought thoughts plot to overthrow poems like governments i can comprehend no more than today despite insubstantial effort i throw over each poem across the governmental divide distilling poems about depressing governments makes me forget the pain of government i can no longer walk among poems or expect much of the government which continues to oppress me as much as poetry tho i expect future censorship of my thoughts may in fact govern poetry

        falling short of useful questions
        a prosthetic for my ripped up heart
        the snow creates a lapse
        in crude town feelings

        a prosthetic for my ripped up heart
        and value-free science
        in crude town feelings
        as if by an invisible hand

        and value-free science
        still paying the rent
        as if by an invisible hand
        moving capital around the globe

my eyelids became untidy

while balancing on satellite
dishes stuck in plastic

my daughter sold into slavery duststorm
in winter

poems with hoof and mouth

disease missing and presumed dead
                      or maybe detained for questioning
                      and clearing landmines words

        slowly emerging from my body

applause junkie embedded in social media
in the presence of absence domain
forever eludes

voices of those we have made other
available if still contingent
life of teleprompted holding pattern patrons
and skies full of dangerous hardware

awaken in machinery

gleaming dust

i pay no attention

to murky motive

leaping in front of a car

hath a dumb language

consistent with language found at the scene

of the crime

this poem is too fictional

no actual person or place is depicted

        permanent smile of the dolphin

corkline at the edge of the net

        grim tasks of survival do not bring happiness

yet the wind

    factory doors

           ringing bells in a corridor

     speaking to song and

hammering a shadow

FLUX (2013)

A postcard which never turns up, wedged under a frayed door, obscured by a dusty wooden table leg, in an abandoned house about to be foreclosed. A postcard forgotten or never sent. A postcard only dreamt about. A postcard never written, but rehearsed until somebody goes mad, featuring a mysterious old stone building with a starving child in front of it wearing a red torn sweater on a post-war street with large grey potholes. A postcard which can never be written, to which ink won't adhere, refused by a post office due to profanity or insufficient postage (may I recite the catalog of insufficiencies?) whose stamps fell off or which dropped into a grey gutter during a recent typhoon (like this one) instead of the mail carrier's white pouch and falls out of holes in dirty red bent metal mailboxes. A postcard with an illegible address, addressed to or by someone in a non-existent country, like this one, written by somebody dead (as dead as the non-existent doorknobs on the fusuma dividing us) perhaps myself....

walking my imaginary
dog and pretending to make
dinner i avoid looking at

sad buildings because
the world has suddenly turned
quite somber

i would like to liberate
the past from the future
for the sake of all

fallen people
though you can't get up
up the song rises

as if to meet someone
a group of demonstrators
red sun in my eyes

a sense of home evades you
and today the world seemed to be just a scene
and my true self merely my subconscious

talking to strangers
eating tasteless food
it's never a happy ending

       in a sealed cave
       black night
       stranger to words

       drowsy branch
       strangely warm
       honey and wine

       glorious reign
       a cup of miniature
       sorting the gleam

dirty pillow
no one has used
restless and familiar

in the nomenclature
by which stars multiply
irreducible fragments

the lake's mirror
clear and transparent
darkening fruit wilderness

together and alone
item found on the carpet
once surprised me

nothing to do
filling a broken drawer
tower hides mountain

on a long stroll
legs become stone
windows reflect neon

silent field
overwhelms the day
waving weakly

blurred skyline
disturbed by birds
a sliding of angles

exhaust fumes
one eyed cat
things i've seen

yellow parchment
under my wing
endless night

orange butterfly
the terrifying self
continually windblown

covered with cold
unsafe conditions
my shoulder drops

immigration office
blonde girl in sparkly clothes
in broad daylight

a single word
bits of trash
call my name

ground merges with buildings
on a deserted street
a sky becomes language

The shop was a mess of confused color and noise. The day will shine. Cherry blossoms unmasked hidden wounds in the tired metropolis. So I jumped out and ran across two intersections. In the middle of your bursts of laughter. My favorite tree lived in the park. Yours was.

Cherry blossoms unmask hidden words in the tuneful metropolis. Critique is ultimately respectful. Ideas lead to the fractured I and the dissolved self.

There is no love which does not begin with the revelation of a possible world. The more consciousness the more despair is always merrier. Critique ultimately discarded.

This culture happened by accident. We don't expect the aid of a waking for this is not a dream. Having a self and an eternal (fractured) self. Ideas lead us to a fissured metropolis hidden by laughing trees.

A person's resiliency can be measured by the power to forget. Full of screams and crying. Yours was. The park was a mass of conflated jumping within intersections.

The dark will triumph. So I slept in and waited for the power to forget. Full of dissolves and scrapings by. This resiliency which never happened. There is no word which does not begin with the improbability of love.

Whoever is careless with the truth in small matters cannot be trusted with important matters.
Albert Einstein

of all in the world
which could be absent
and never far
that will be missed
though i am foreign
& have forgotten all the words

of the tiny words
caught in the smaller world
which tend to be foreign
the days i was absent
you may not miss
when reason may be far

thus far
when there are not words
i cannot be Miss
World
though reason may be absent
and always foreign

to not know what is foreign
a common state is far
people tend to appear absent
due to rearranging the words
if only the world
could be missing

would it be amiss
to hide all things foreign
because the world
which can be seen from afar
is not trapped in words
nor despite intentions absent

a separate self is absent
like a target you miss
a unit like words
from outside the foreign
body or far
from the world

though the absent world
may be foreign words will be missed
and safe if from afar

<spring>

It's time to start something new
like a headache that lasts for months

and you want to give to someone else
that person in your imagination who

betrayed you but stands now by the
bed holding your slippers

Do not walk on this product
unless directed to do so by a medical practitioner

but it's ok if you give the dog a boner
while watching the cherry blossoms

which the wind will tear to bits tomorrow
in future false memories

\<summer\>

Because the summer is delicate
we can deconstruct it easily

replacing it with old movies
where endings are always

supplied arbitrarily
by overpaid producers

In your annihilated bones
I pass unopened fountains

where the world empties
onto a sea of stone

thinking of cash crops I could grow
resembling substances like tobacco

teenagers drop from car windows
as job creation for clean up crews

\<autumn\>

Aesthetic distance
implies temporary detachment from the pressures

of the world in which a reader lives in order
to enter the secondary world

that which I am making now
now that leaves are required to be countably additive

in this fashion falling leaves are another
cover for financial collapse

\<winter\>

A painting depicting a winter scene
may be better than the real thing

The great artistic achievements
of prehistoric Europe are impersonal

and the language has run out of words
There will be no more snow

cuz that statute of limitations too
has run out

dominate flattened hills for
      pathways to neurons
lost in dispersions of language
      lining up the numbers
everything you know is wrong
      arrabiatta bazooka sukiyaki at which i aim
if it was coded i did not know the key
      in the meantime voices

           still trembling devouring light
           violent imprint of my mother
           any particular thought at the back of my head
           public garden with nappy grass

robust babe shot of sympathy certain amusements
eyebrows bristling tall buildings crowd together
nobody walks that street anymore

           happy happy an odd sound
           ghost of life in silver miniature
           denouement is hectic prediction
           protect me from the alarm head

the clock is flat and i want it dead
    window a mob memories in the shape of burning planes
dreams unopened terrify you forever oh look pigeons
    on the stairs droppings the only noise
allowed in this cramped world in which
    no one fits unless thrust by force

ignored by clouds tired of repeating happy victim
    remember who you are among very hidden people

tendency to reject tissue not like my own
    oblivion self key to salvation oh patty cake and jonny cake
lay the word on my back so i can shrug it off if you
    are often affected by rashes
conception which we are now outlining allows
    me to cease to adhere
hands in pockets flyaway inflammation spiritual
    cheekbones rustling wildly
mouthful of hands a manner of treating the world in
    detachable forests tho scarcely succeeding
scarcely a scar slut unfold objection time dreamless
    dreary dividing the soul of reason in objective time
things to be left unfinished

        truly hard to kill the parasite
        without also killing the host gaps
        between life and death in
        ambivalent language substitute for inaction
        in the shroud condition of cognition

dear friend. you are finally able to match n with
n. if there was any to be found (no one is
telling). the elderly get out

their coloring books. focus on the test pattern until sleep
becomes yours. the latest

technological breakthrough enables more war. the future is
dark green with no borders. perhaps

the keeper of the fire has been banished. you grip the railing. i
wait for hours in an anonymous city

to turn from object to subject. the i of the
formula. rigid intake control. a lack which

creates desire summons nothing to
itself. consciousness never

confers meaning. a certain conception of being

may be no revelation. to explain why the world
is. my complaint about boredom led to the bank

failure. scandalous truth is on my side so i throw
myself on the floor. yet i am
productive and pay taxes though will
never emerge from this difficulty

surviving another earthquake of absence. but the
language always frightens me. but only if the
infection clears up. voided hands lift my skirt

invisibly in the forest's underbelly. the forest has no
face and cannot jeer when a tree unwinds. nerves
at the edge. our innocent bond is broken. let my

gaze always be medical. an analogous grasp. let there be
mouthpieces. becoming purer with each glass of water.
despite events i did not choose and cannot change.

continuing to be happy in my
unhappy way. all the while i pretend

your clothes. you can tell the street in
paris. clouds were a chain
reaction which cost money. maybe a

flimsy pair of tweezers holds up the sky. however much you
hope. my field of vision is never

tended in the deep seated needs of nuclear
reactors. my bed sticks to me. a puppy wags its
tail furiously even as rocks reach it.

announcing a crack in the containment lead. gag
orders breed funds. consult a doctor if this should
happen to you

earn easy typing income. lather,
rinse, repeat. in a contest
between truth and beauty money wins every

time. model AF6200 is not as good as last year's but
costs more. i may be radioactive iodine. what
remains after the tidal wave. go ask father

nature. somebody stole my vertebrae. your
browsing is history. we are
scientists after all. i worry where my eyes will go

next. and would like to move my hand across that
continent but stop myself

tipped pelvis. hindsight is still sight except when
father time divorces mother nature but not before

begetting father nature whose rage is the length of
a continent and deeper than the ocean. i won't be

getting out much for a while. the heaven i made on earth blew
to pieces. bank blowout. i asked

for a blow dry not a blow job. blank and
blue city. learning nothing

greater than the plumed building.
there are better ways to anger people

than comment on their views. you could
mention their hair for instance

another form of militarized darkness. rationing my thoughts
so there'd be some left for breakfast. i was

wrong. if not so dead i'd call you immediately. even though
clouds frighten me into moving i'm stuck in

tomorrow's tedium. collectively the seasons have much power
but individually we can smash them to

bits. i married a sexy macho man with no
emotions or thoughts. ideology alone in a back room

eclipsed by stars under homeless
lice-infested blankets. able to find no other use for

the pineapple i put it on my head. the poets have left the
building now. whether the past

or future makes me more anxious i'm no longer
sure as i can no longer distinguish them. you said run

for cover so i am hidden by trees. yet the accountant appears
fierce when i turn on the lights. in an email to

me beginning dear sirs

wanting to purchase a secular democracy i forgot to
read the fine print and ended up head of a tobacco

company. later buried at sea i showered with old
money. in the shadow of big banks. i was busy

lawyering up. collective scams leveraged to the
hilt hammer the poor. fake profits put desperation

in the air clouded by large bonuses. we hoped for a
religious apocalypse not an economic one but secret

millionaires brought restless leg syndrome to the skies
creating wage slaves and brand loyalty

to ensure my existence referring to myself in the
third person. and hope it will extend the limits

of treatability. while the
rich avert their eyes. to

manage the unmanageably arid dreams of
toxicologists where no crops grow. an unsafe dose of

language was released when i accidentally
damaged a safety valve. i get a physical when

i finish my tour. evil twin theory is a sucker
punch for lost gutter types merely following orders

though in full compliance with
federal law. since all languages

have unknown side effects. doomed to
fail the reality tests again and again. death by

misadventure. given random privately
funded trials. extending patents by creating new

diseases befitting the drugs. pending further
investigations. the way the world

works. with small incisions

to exhume the linguistic body. we wish for the
poem's safe return. into the arms of goddesses. tho

i suspect trees are really stencils lurking in my
private eye. enemies which can't be seen. crowds

aren't enough. words and sky empty
themselves. i could have been a contender

or a key witness. some things
cannot be translated

   into the exact opposite

         queen without a city

upon the self itself

     becoming no self

vanishing

         over something earthy

   wanting to become

an experimental god

   on which the canvas or

     a temple for instance

earth moves as if bitten

  escapes

        border almost on

    finished building dissolves

apart from the self

        becoming the canvas

nailed to such restriction

      a part of the self

           at all existence

   as great as this

     could

cannot be removed or separated

   and besides

                from the earth

          when the guilty are many

   numerous sentences

      updated

              eternity in head

whatever happened   from

         the side of reason
     plucked

   silence moving in air

inserted building is

                latticework of dissolving thought

        recovered

        hollow form is   divine stroll

overblown

            floats in my eye

       the temple

in an attempt   independent of

                  time   lesson

        in retired space

     enshrined like gauze

     wrapped around your hand
     cannot stop

behind   every landscape a self

     coast moves

                intent on something

                    which cannot be plucked

from prayer

           delicate code   disappearing partially

                     in sea mist

             for example

desire is consistent

             with the swapped temple

on the ground   what we made

             swabbed   in air

Chapter 1

She had never spoken, she did not speak. Quiet, quiet. She sat on the stairs, the beige carpet. Waiting. For what…

Chapter 2

The light was beige like the carpet. Always. It seemed so. Her mother interrupted her just as Ken was raping Barbie. *What are you doing?* She didn't know…

Recalling this the day Tiger Woods admitted to having an affair. Many affairs.

She found the city quite ugly. But after she met him she found it beautiful.

Chapter 3

(It had only been her therapist that had been bullied.)

Yet she suspected her sister had borderline personality disorder. Thinking perhaps something was wrong with herself. Maybe not. But… was it a sin to be sensitive – better to be callous as a serial killer? Serial killers who like the therapist had been bullied in childhood. She had cleaned the convents on weekends and received free ice cream after, though sometimes only a popsicle.

She gradually could overcome the men in her life, she thought.

There was the guy who went out to get money and never returned. He had asked her: *Why do you like me?* She didn't know. He had picked her and that was that.

She didn't know if she minded that his other girlfriend worked as a stripper. In the room over the strip club, his room, she sat on his face, when he asked her to. *Don't you feel anything?* There was nothing – she didn't know why – as the neon blinked into the beige carpeted living room.

Chapter 4

There was the rock star or would be rock stars – actually there were several men that fit this description. One whose real love was heroin. Another whose real love was probably himself or maybe just music. Another like the one just mentioned. These two similar guys were friends. She had intended to sleep with the second one not the first one. But the first guy chose her first. She went along with it.

This happened twice, with other musicians. The one she liked did not pick her so she went home with his friend. A year later she broke up with the friend who was always lying, asking her for money for the bus when she had none, and pretending not to be sleeping with the Asian foreign student who answered the phone at his dorm. *She just gets tired and sleeps here sometimes.* That was the end of it. He was always asking for bus fare. The kitchen floor was always dirty. When the toilet broke, the landlord – who once drunkenly reached for her breast when she went to complain about the mice – suggested she must have put cat litter in there.

A year later still she slept with the friend but just one time. He was enamored of the dancers he collaborated with. She was not a dancer. She was not sure if she was pretty or not. Her dancing skill was average. Maybe briefly around the age of 25. All women are pretty at that age. She had hoped he would stay longer. It was just one time. He told her not to get up when he left early in the morning. So she went back to bed. His relatives made very good Middle Eastern food.

The guy who invited her to Passover dinner with the long neck. There were a lot of Jewish boyfriends. Most were single. She remembered hiding behind a wall when a wife appeared in elegant clothes at the expensive ski resort and her first orgasm which the wife's husband had given her – how the ripples went over her. She thought she was dying. She remembered him making sly remarks to their boss at the accounting firm and the boss asking *Are you two involved?* and him smiling sheepishly.

After he left she found the city quite ugly again. She believed she had become the phantom of the opera stalking an invisible enemy.

CHAPTER 5

There was the guy who wanted her to scream *Fuck me hard.* She was afraid, so she complied. She was grateful when he left early the next morning and she never heard from him again.

There was the guy who set their things on fire.

The young, handsome actor showed her a picture of an eighty-year old woman saying it was his other girlfriend. Later she showed up drunk at a bar where he was working as he talked loudly to his friend about how he liked to come between a woman's tits. She knew her own tits were not big enough for that.

The guy who waited for her in an alley, dragged her face down by her feet, and after whacking her in the head repeatedly stuffed her into a car she was able to jump out of when he took his hand off her for a minute while driving. She fell on all fours on the pavement and just as she was getting up to run, his hand grazed her left ankle. He gave up though. He would have caught her if he had tried harder. Maybe she wasn't worth it. She ran home with one shoe on. It was a cheap black cotton shoe with tan rubber sole she had found at the imported Chinese goods store. The next day she could not find the shoe in the alley. Her blue t-shirt had been torn to shreds and the red marks of his fingers on her arm lasted for several days. Though this was years ago she could still see them. The police would not listen when she said he was a tall white man she had never met. They did not listen to the white part or the part about his being a stranger rather than an old lover.

There was the relative who enticed her into bed a few times.

There was the policeman who attacked her in the car after giving her a ride home from work. And the policeman who called her for a date repeatedly after her reporting the robbery; she thought the robber was probably the young landlord who had visited her once. It was hard to get him to leave, just like the police – they wanted to stay and watch the fight. That apartment was shabby too and that landlord ripped off a rare record of hers. He probably was also the person who stole the drugs. She had never slept with him.

She often watched fights with the guy who burned their things.

The Xray technician who refused to give her a hospital gown told her she had to walk naked to the Xray machine. The medical students laughed as she walked from one end of the long room to the other shivering with her arms crossed over her pale sunken chest and her head bowed. On a different day the nurses laughed while she screamed in pain as they shot air into her fallopian tubes.

Chapter 6

It was time to decide her career. The clippings arranged haphazardly on the floor. A large cockroach was running over them. Then another, then another.

Thinking about her future made her hungry. She grabbed the cast iron skillet, which was heavy in her hand. As the oil started sizzling, cockroaches started jumping into the pan from the painted white cabinets above. The building had once been a hotel.

She woke up when her cat was tossing a mouse up and down on her stomach on the futon. The next morning she found its flattened body under a book near a red stain on the carpet. Her other lazy cat just sat and watched.

One of her cats had extra digits. The other was fat and cried a lot.

She decided to start keeping a diary. She wrote on the cover of the notebook 'The Nightmare Journals.' Lizards criss-crossed the walls. Then another, then another.

CHAPTER 7

Her illness kept her from the new career. In the hospital the orderlies reminded her of old boyfriends. She dreamed her death was peaceful.

She was no longer sure if the city was ugly or beautiful.

CHAPTER 8

A bicycle arrived but she couldn't assemble it. Free shipping had been included. She arranged the coupons in alphabetical order. There was little money, but pop corn was cheap. Her sister gave her a painting of two girls knifing each other in a pink and blue kitchen. Her kitchen was yellow but she knew one of the girls was herself.

CHAPTER 9

She began to lose track of time, of places, of people. Earthquakes seemed to mimic her
moods and tidal waves washed away her thoughts.

Different kinds of radiation lead to different illnesses she read. She began speaking a language no one else spoke.

At that time of course it was called the gay cancer. He had warned her that he was bisexual, after they had sex.

She had always hoped to be a drag queen, but…

Chapter 10

The stock market was plummeting. Another oil spill threatened wildlife in the area. Her high school friend wore so much mascara that her eyes looked like black spiders. She had called them 'balderdash' because they dashed after they balled you. He was the first to take her virginity. A few weeks before had not led to sex though the other girl sucked her nipple during the strip poker game. Her boyfriend freaked out so that ended the game. The 'balderdash' often played air hockey in the local arcade, near the Kmart where her mother bought her clothes, though she lied, saying that the clothes came from a more upscale place.

Chapter 11

Memories tend to get fuzzy over time. The mice had fuzzy heads.

Another guy had simply gone on vacation and never called her when he got back in town. She walked the streets near his house for weeks hoping to bump into him. Later she found he had moved to a different part of the city. He sent her a letter about his alcoholic parents. That summer was quite hot.

Some kid had killed his parents with a gun he found at his grandparent's house. Her father had always carefully folded the paper bag which carried his lunch to work before putting it neatly in a drawer.

There was now a more serious threat of nuclear radiation. Radiant was how she was described in the prom dress many years ago. She was hopeful. *Unutterable omens would sing her home.*

So long as the skyline remains
obscure I can feel calm. Although in the
same room I call you long distance as
the color leaves my face and enters
the bureaucrat's painting. Though
the garden is now dissolving the insects
in flames create a pattern resembling
last year's sofa the same size as the
crashed plane overhead. Always
I leave home as if to find a new
one. My body may be said to be
alive to the extent to which its parts
are functioning. One difficulty was
in deciding which of the many
physical forces involved were
important and which could be
safely ignored. Even snow
flakes obey mathematical
laws. The degree to which despair
rises. Flowers may mimic the
forces inside attempting to
annihilate each other. In order
to comply with the spirits
found in a body cavity
search we placed all politicians
in quarantine to protect
the public sector

Walking outside, hoping the air may be better. The air hops with me. I think of the mail unopened and the unanswered phone. Would it be better to wait in the stale air for the phone or inside the metal box for the mail? Is it better to

perfect oneself alone in the dark or desecrate oneself in public? When does the outside become dirty and limiting, muddied by base desire – or is it the inside that is filthy? Though I know I must flee from the machines eating everyone at the office, even though severely admonished for

not staying til all my limbs are gone. So with all my limbs, forced to join a doomsday cult where we are asked to sacrifice a limb in order to approximate the masses, yet, I do not, being too selfish (angry?) to give up anything, move alone toward the end of history.

Though my eyes are scattered I can hide the emptiness within with a vermilion coat and blue eyelashes. No one will notice that Milton's light has dimmed. I put a verb under every umbrella in case you feel like running. The temple is supposed to mean something but nobody is sure. I thought the cherry blossoms though torn and dirty would last all year but the wind swept through the house knocking over father's funeral photograph. I know I am supposed to stay under a heavy object such as a major appliance. If you pluck a grey hair by its roots doves appear the next day. But that is the ending to last year's story. Even if a wound looks like a freshly ploughed field I cannot feel responsible for your

lost baggage. The truth is I am allergic to everything red and blue, and worry anti-depressants will ruin the sun's melancholia. But I could still watch it from afar while pretending to smile. I hope the sea may be colder than ever and know once I submerge my toe in it it won't come back. Silly to believe birds know the best way to fly to the beach.

Skin cancer is the goddess' revenge on the vain and foolish. Just because I've said it doesn't mean it's not true. Sunlight tries to squeeze into every room but fails. The house I grew up in was a dark cave even though my parents were wealthy. The dog was let out every Sunday. How foolish to return. I am more afraid of happiness than I am of the sun's anger. I

would like to liven up each house with a piece of rotting fish stolen from the temple. If the lighthouse is painted pink I'll no longer be allergic to it and when the sun resembles caramel latte I'll finally move. I'd suggest birds prefer the sea to the sun but the wind would argue. Even if I am a man so old I can scarcely carry the newspaper to the trash bin. If the

drum is beaten with a stick somebody will answer the telephone though my slippers are missing and none of this is actually visible from the lighthouse.

awful stillness
hide me forever
cleave my native tongue, funeral flowers

shadow of trees
the wind is dry mist rolls
cover my head in a thick fog

failing to learn the language of
the rulers but singing the
song of the dispossessed:

oh the background is out of focus
ah men in suits read comic strips thin and wan
colonial inheritance is a pretty garden

in my rucksack hidden
in the self conscious air
where money may be time

white dust torn fields
meaning shrinks sublime
in the empty seat

at the drive in movie
the film I can't see continues
my poem is complete to the extent i am not

like a stranger
a new script
here there are
buckets of hysteria

a road an auditorium
a parade of surfaces
an expression
given to you in passing

the spot which remains
once you're gone
before imagination
makes us frail

once a lake
a simple knot for
a fluttering day
is creased

wildblacklake (2014)

goodbyes precede every hello
overtones of sky
festival of dolls and
wisteria of calligraphy

interiors on a pale surface
the mind becomes quiet
a rosy contraption
beyond what logic can endure

falling objects
denuded bone
texture of documents
resounding voyage

*

important news
a car a mountain path
her upturned face
few casualties

narrow hallway
holding its breath squeezes past
alone me not still
amid planes

vast emptiness
a kind but chilly harbor
stubborn mountains
arise from nothing

the wind outside the mind
post mortem
angle of endless teeth
resurrect the quivering sun

protected by the forest
a doll trapped in the house
my arm twisted
things to do

smoothing of space
millions of morals
womb for words
see enclosed brochure

*

elegant bird
under automobile tires
replying eagerly
a sun sinks

ambushed breasts
in wild silence
wintry carnival
of social systems

silhouette in a window
the night overtakes
waiting for a sign
becomes increasingly still

Distant Landscapes (2015)

The breathing outside my labored mine.
Heavens in bits.
Roots in mental cavities.
Soft, soft the painting of blue.
Becoming ruined cities of crystallized air.
Nervous dialogue. Solemn child, grime wavers.
Sudden funeral for me. Empty tedious steps.
A little left. Too late.

No object is money. A lonely place of rocks and sand. In dreams a sense of deafness. Falling in innocent silence.

All foreplay is glitch. A trick of my subconscious. I'm frozen you're dead. Twisting wisteria.

Mistress mind cult of prehistoric notorious phonetic
Mammary fiction rice sack hysteria compilation perception
Deathless wall freezes gaze judicial penetration
Unlimited cigarette fantasies of identity disjunctive
    compilation
Audience of corpses by oceans endowed conglomerate
    instrument
Enclosed body undying fashion shrunken night

    burrowing in the earth   to find a real world
        beneath the fictitious ones

          walking into ruin   damaged birds
move   thru an eccentric sky

to grasp a feeling of home
              of a secret reverberating self
this is not an exit

<echo poetics>

I become the tree tho it does not become me. Each branch of a temporarily retrieved memory of a hypersensitive poet with a stormy personality blown apart by tonight's rain. Down the street workmen build a house in the forest for the wealthy, eating lunch in dirty trucks shoes off white stockinged feet hanging out car windows ramen in styrofoam cups and throwaway chopsticks. It's impossible to know the forest's prerequisites. A large owl flies over the young grass the plump brown rabbit ate yesterday. The poem finally accepts the reverberations of the forest. There's an operatic grammar to be found among birds and insects, but language cannot stop to find it. The hills only appear to be tragic. One glance is never enough. How the forest haunts me. Each night I dream a blade of grass. My heart becomes hollow and everything becomes wilderness. It's precisely here where my thoughts turn to plywood.

unknown person in the person
tree in the tree
voice only i could hear
forest unable to look in my direction

when does a forest stop being a forest?
a frantic search ensued
for the lost language/identity/girl/animal
she likes the scenery

in the dark you can't see anything
(that's what she likes about it)
tree like an erect male organ
tho minding my own business

disappointment of the forest
his mystery
marshland of poetic toxicology
photoplay of flying objects

binding contract
used as directed in a safehouse
when i wake
will winter begin

voiceless sound
if i stay here long enough
empty moment
a rabbit draws near and comes back

flowers too white
hollow point
ambient whirlwind
pity parties

mystery cascade
floating fingertips
damaged branch
my body still present

a house a bird a
village where no one is
laughing bones
flickering face of the sea

it's strange to think
at all
about the poor
a pure line

in the direction of the abyss
one moment
another precinct in the mind
renders a landscape fragile

the wind flutters
on a need to know basis
false diagnosis of sound
the sky is mine

swept away like blank lines
brief description of clouds
hurts the horizon
taking the world away

tower burning
look of attention on my face
merely the tree at hand
daily images recorded

we all run to the window
a scene analyzed
later than expected
made to disappear

singingly in dead languages
all of suffering humanity
suddenly seems old
blunting the horizon

glass ceiling of the forest
row of strange flowers
behind a fence
in a grove opening and closing

shrinking the horizon
an inner life outside
vulgar studio appearing in a photograph
poorly constructed magical trances

to grasp a feeling of home
spread of animals
i was not deemed structurally sound
turning over an old leaf

my fake life part of a low fence
all secretions
toxins from my skin
protons decay

reinventing an ocean
appetite for grass
broad lines of plains
visible breath

in the theatre of nature
stillness of a moment
chuffing tiger
hidden in language

dwelling in anger
spilling out among leaves
melting away of the self
holding the forest together bends

my body a foreigner belonging to me
a sewer rat
coerced confession
using only my inner tongue

eternal taste of the forest
groping for more portraiture
ruffian geography
identifies with sky

distraction zones
up and down pine needles
in a spine
a river a mouth replaying

yearning vanishes
thought remains at a distance
shattering of words
catastrophe of trees

partitioning of my body
in fake hands
failure of the forest
to prevent further yearning

bird outside my window
landscape lingers in my
bones gradually
emptied of music

i was limited to black and white

rates in parenthesis

walking on glass rivers

a small room in the sea

hidden in those legs

the space of summer

a labyrinth of language

my small house

white flowers

green thoughts

sleep wantonly in decadent leaves

look at each stadium fade

the head of a woman

a prologue of sound

nothing rhymes with me
my body transparent as the sea

my mind rain dripping from the roof
moment eloquent with meaning

pale as a corpse
presentiment of the richest idea

but what happens
my earlier conception of life

i live on emptiness
an event which remains hidden

for a long time
imperfections in the narrative

nothing more than thought
not even an echo

Developing relationships
With what is normally impossible

tiny as to be non-existent. Ancestor worship.

Exegesis.

Every froth. The aching of today. Methods
of refraction. Peppered with doom. Mystery is the
hell. Unending horizon. Limpid dance.
Ambiguous strands. Analogous solitude. Seen as
exile. Buried doubt. A boneless moon. So tiny as
to be.

diurnal (2016)

(1)

(and) where is my mouth
the day you became

part of my skin
a whole fragment

needy telephone eyes
smile in the dark

sing! sweet chariot
of deceased dreaming shadows

pointing towards zero
fluted/carbonated metaphors

showcase of distractions
a succession of coarseness

erase the chimes of regret
of dying flowerbeds

(8)

to translate the clouds
above ugly buildings

books on my body
strange amounts of granite

gradual shading
is nobody's theory

sifting seasons and plastic creatures
plummeting consciousness

icy lake
comatose to lifeless

devouring itself
a balancing of lines

chaste marriage
both surface and subtext

(10)

unfinished sketch
duplications of goddesses

in case of earthquakes
black ivory some green

ambivalent critique
lost on a mountain

the necessity of the unnecessary
conversation among trees

traveling to change
what one's eyes see

chemistry folklore
extravagant plain

sprouting from my head
a non-existent sky

(21)

my head a vase
my face a footrest

my neck a thud
my arm a whammy

your eye a wrapper
your back a tool

your face a shrine
your toe a morsel

our torso a shrapnel
our brain champagne

our ribs obtuse
our skull whiplash

their bone awhirl
there bones a world

(22)

covert operations
such a world

dry landscape
nailed to a wall

firewall of love
the horizon disappears

long list of errors
plastic flower wreath

dotted lines
facts not in evidence

despite the living
wet pine

the body's harmony
a ruffled wind

(23)

weary of platitudes
undressing in front of a window

most of what we knew was wrong
sweeping the sidewalk endlessly

new worlds are created
using a dead language ultimately becoming stone

suffocated by portrait accents
surrounding us like shrieking planets

closely watched marching in your mind
too far down the path to be seen

added to culture subtracted from the soul
shadows of an eastern day

across a tortured garden
a length of longing

terra form[a] (2017)

slow pull towards silence
shifting frames of reference
i'd do anything to be alone
dark corridor

dreamy landscapes with flowing boundaries
messy undulations in my head
dying from invisible wounds
silent and distant

guided by reasoning
perfect sounds emit, evaporate
at the edge of the alphabet
glimpse of expatriate emotion

next to a sullen cross
meandering on dulled skin
fixated on school uniforms
blades of interior

moving past quivering darkness
eye in the forest
colliding wooden park bench
not even a raised skirt

to match an eyebrow
wilted flower code
assault upon language
both sides of a coin

yellow and black
false dilemma on an empty train
images faster than an eye
palm trees in a row of sorrow

no one speaks
of bark of sunlight
a man whimpers at the clouds
somewhere a young girl

plastic flowers in a pink bedroom
my back crooked from watching
yellow barges in pushing away sense
in a portable landscape

stars trapped in nets
dire thrown carelessly
diced food
dark web of buildings

in a summer heat of reason
split open like a moving variegated shadow
across a black canvas
are pink lines

weblike forest
yellowed lips of sense
against a moving
target of glitter trees

thoughts leftover
soundless atmosphere
slow move away from fading language
to which i pin my hope

great blur of reason
new versions of radiant forests
at the deaf of feeling
a hundred views of

outdated throng of random listening
dissolve into grey pools of regret
yellow objects in my mind
not this heavy lifting of concrete

enigmatic grave in the text
walk ending in madness
lopsided form of balance
dispensing reason

sleeping on damaged flowers
we walked all night
in the city where he was beating her
lack of symmetry

planets line up
for easy handling
thrust deep within
my stale vagina

torn streets and bent houses
in a fragile past
terraced cemetery
permitting no passage

bundle of sticks
hurriedly on the surface
sterile bed of consoling trees
words belonging to the earth

wreckage of human existence
innermost doll
yellow tulips
against a black fence

words of leaves
lopsided bag of weeds
mirror text
floral scission

shrub of memory
in the failing arms of another other
dull shard of language
pierces me

incomprehensible stammering of trees
impossible dialogue
rubble of words
rips floral utterance to foreground

hesitant walk on a moor
historic encounters with large feet
leading away from homeland
inaccessible impoverished language

incoherent forest struck by
metaphysical lightning

beloved murders
shrines without temples
linguistic bodies
never recovered

fatal homage
between theory and a world
however i think
a tomb of poetry

without their faces
aesthetically limited due to their

preoccupation with sociology (that pseudoscience!)
all the while promoting the dominant culture's

    mainstream values: a culture that has arisen around this

    ideal represented indiscriminately as violent

criminals – love relationships are just
not that important (however one feels)

    about it – a form of dependence was always

    there, signifiers with no referents

– to some people this appears to be a limitation

(not looking at me when i talk to you
the violin is a difficult instrument

that speaks loudly and slowly with exaggerated gestures
for a homecoming with no home

    living fossil in a barren environment in which
    few survive

grotesque restlessness of recovery amplified
by temporary promises, a carefully worded bed, tantrum
after our fling of bling. Your beloved turbulent
voice of escape. A predatory building lost in
dwindling twilight

in a once innocent landscape, whining while meditating,
an asian apocalypse flowers into an inexhaustible
body mural, after centuries of naked ache, lessons
in unreal silence. Ruled by ordinary horizons,
thanks very much, foreplay for embossed messages
scrawled on the backs of the overworked and disfigured,
a master of invalidation, improved weaponry, *my little country
speaking to me from behind a wall*

face of a samurai on a sofa cushion. A holistic mode of thought labelled madness. The tiny space I'm allowed, garments which prevent action. My mouth falls between my thighs and screams.

logic of the swamp. Dark, troubled past stripped of meaning. A self-oppressing mother. Living cadaver in chaotic topology. Blood-stained persons.

quasi cause, certain bonds (or not). Limited returns. Antidote to intimacy. Lost cities. Collective amnesia. The weight of decay on my tongue.

deleted and swollen. Words go where they want. On a small patch of land. A pulsation swallowed by multiple horizons. Associated associative disorders.

[paperwork fantasies]

three narrow buildings
incandescent with rage

unrepaired bridge
falls into a concrete-walled stream

perpetually scratching the surface
my lost country

scraps of language
inside myself a lost child waving

thin fabric
in perpetual heat

the high seas
assume a wrongful place at a throne

swallowed by green land
distracted by faint traces of lack

wind composing obituaries for silent birds
i feel a blade

of grass on my neck blue
flowers sprout from fissures in my skin

(what type of flower does not matter)

talking points of
sprawling space

becomes faint(er and fainter)
with tiring hands

to feel young again in a different field
with money which grew narrower in grammar

breathing fast, his soft waist
gradual accidents befall

swatting at darkness pretending
we are strangers

the truth of appearances
fade monthly, end reluctantly

unnecessary surfaces are always masterpieces

at 45 degree angles
bent over the table, more furniture

vile and hypnotic
soothing me like nothing else

bodily harm and strips of dull silver
in the word 'prescription'

how long will my spirit
end badly

half a person equals political malaise
lost in an interior life

absentee poets objectify myself
erase the cityscape

ghost ship in brackish water
wayward thought

phenomenological corset
pollution and contagion

hesitation wound
shoot fish in a barrel

engulfed cities between day and night
example of silence

fallen world [intermittent in my landscape]
identify with cliffs

migrant crisis
days too long

who messed up the story line
embedded in wrongdoing

how long will my spirit be
residual dew of you

checkpoint disasters
(although i'm dying my persona's thriving)

remote possibilities of escape

a person in pain exceeds language

inventing herself and watching herself [die]

i cannot recall events

as what happens is what feels untrue

& belongs nowhere & walks endlessly

if nothing tangible is at stake

mornings in bed, mostly alone

into this disfigurement

    conversing with corpses

  mumbling beside

mimesis of unfathomed archetypes

      as a rigid joint

  at the bottom of a wastebasket

        each word its own planet

        haunting the body

merging of potential shapes

        in elusive pools

during a test run

        that would become a life

biofuel   or stage symbol

what becomes undone   or lurks beneath

my frozen heart   her upturned body

a set of relation

        (has no language)

moving images

        audible, lie in wait

my heart in italics again

        glance through me

                your hand and its shadow

faraway snow

        breathes

in your mouth

        forgotten letters

singed with grief

                    if not for

              the finest of feeling

covered in silence

                       another eye behind an eye

talking to a wall

                             rapid edge

branches in brown bundles twisted with rope

              create a fence

                             around an anonymous house

darkening

      a forest grows thick around us

as indented song

          erases the skin

leaving only grey bone

          i place my foot at the entrance

              to the house and wait there

in a corner of a park

        a child with blonde hair

      her parents are gone

(I never asked for these eyes, this skin)

under the same heavy thatched roof

                look, let's talk about the future

so close it's gone

fading flower the air is crisp face in a mirror

sudden light trudging through the forest cicada on its back

youthful memories bicycles racing by filth on concrete with
                                                        yellow leaves

a dead insect lands on my vagina footprints lost in deep snow

    joyful trend

           crocheted sky

    strange quiet sunlight

        rustle of curtains moving

           flooded street

www.ingramcontent.com/pod-product-compliance
Lightning Source LLC
Chambersburg PA
CBHW031629160426
43196CB00006B/335